WE FEED A DEER

ANN HUGHES

with revisions by Betty Modaressi

Illustrated by
Suzanne Snider

Open Court
La Salle, Illinois

The idea for this storybook was suggested by the work of Amy Thorleifson and Dory Hodgson of Edmonds School District No. 15, Lynnwood, Washington.

OPEN COURT and ✹ are registered in the U.S. Patent and Trademark Office.

Printed in the United States of America

ISBN 0-8126-1002-4

We're free!

We see a real deer.
We meet the deer.

"Here, feel these."

3

"See the deer's feet."

4

"See the rear feet."

The deer sees the seeds.
He eats the seeds.

He sees these weeds.
He eats the weeds.

"See the deer's teeth."

The deer's near a tree.
He sees a leaf.
He eats the leaf.

We'll feed the deer a leaf.
"Here, deer.
See the leaf.
Eat the leaf."

The deer eats the leaf.

We see seeds.
We'll feed the deer these seeds.
He'll eat these seeds.

12

We lead the deer.

14